# THE INSIDER'S GUIDE TO FISHING

# SALTWATER FISHING
## LIKE A PRO

### Theia Lake

Published in 2024 by The Rosen Publishing Group, Inc.
2544 Clinton Street, Buffalo, NY 14224

Copyright © 2024 by The Rosen Publishing Group, Inc.

Portions of this work were originally authored by Mary-Lane Kamberg and published as *Saltwater Fishing*. All new material in this edition was authored by Theia Lake.

Editor: Greg Roza
Designer: Michael Flynn

All rights reserved. No part of this book may be reproduced in any form without permission in writing from the publisher, except by a reviewer.

**Cataloging-in-Publication Data**

Names: Lake, Theia.
Title: Saltwater fishing like a pro / Theia Lake.
Description: New York : Rosen Publishing, 2024. | Series: The insider's guide to fishing | Includes glossary and index.
Identifiers: ISBN 9781499476064 (pbk.) | ISBN 9781499476071 (library bound) | ISBN 9781499476088 (ebook)
Subjects: LCSH: Saltwater fishing--Juvenile literature.
Classification: LCC SH457.L35 2024 | DDC 799.16--dc23

Some of the images in this book illustrate individuals who are models. The depictions do not imply actual situations or events.

*Manufactured in the United States of America*

CPSIA Compliance Information: Batch #CWRYA24. For further information, contact Rosen Publishing at 1-800-237-9932.

# CONTENTS

INTRODUCTION . . . . . . . . . . . . . . . . . . . . . . . . . 4

## CHAPTER 1
PREPARING TO FISH . . . . . . . . . . . . . . . . . . . . 6

## CHAPTER 2
GRAB YOUR GEAR! . . . . . . . . . . . . . . . . . . . . . 20

## CHAPTER 3
START FISHING! . . . . . . . . . . . . . . . . . . . . . . 34

## CHAPTER 4
MAKE YOUR CATCH . . . . . . . . . . . . . . . . . . . . 48

## CHAPTER 5
FISH RESPONSIBLY . . . . . . . . . . . . . . . . . . . . 62

GLOSSARY . . . . . . . . . . . . . . . . . . . . . . . . . . . 74

FOR FURTHER READING . . . . . . . . . . . . . . . . 75

FOR MORE INFORMATION . . . . . . . . . . . . . . 76

INDEX . . . . . . . . . . . . . . . . . . . . . . . . . . . . . . 78

ABOUT THE AUTHOR/CONSULTANT . . . . . . . 80

# INTRODUCTION

Picture yourself on a boat out at sea. The wind is in your hair. The waves lap against the sides of your vessel. The scent of salt water perfumes the air. You're filled with eager anticipation, waiting to feel a tug at the end of your line. Finally, you feel it! You grasp your rod tightly, struggling to reel in the animal that's thrashing wildly on your hook! The fight could be over in seconds, the fish swimming away unharmed. Or you might just be able to master this catch, reeling in a trophy fish far bigger than you ever imagined. If this scene appeals to your sense of adventure, then saltwater fishing might be the sport for you!

Each year, millions of people take to the water to try their hand at saltwater fishing. It is an active sport that's uniquely challenging and inspiring. Saltwater fishing takes many different forms and can be practiced from land, on boats, and far out to sea. Types of saltwater fishing include backwater fishing, pier fishing, surf fishing, and deep-sea fishing. Each has its own appeal and drawbacks, and each is best suited to a certain type of catch.

What sets saltwater fishing apart from other kinds of fishing? For one thing, it's usually much faster paced! Some popular saltwater fish include cod, halibut, marlin, sailfish, shark, and tuna. These species usually grow to be much larger than freshwater fish. Many have teeth too! Having larger, more dangerous catches means that saltwater fishing is full of action and excitement.

This person is surf fishing. Surf fishing is practiced right on the edge of the ocean, where the water meets the shore.

In this book, you'll learn all you need to know about the rules of saltwater fishing and how to practice water safety. You'll discover what gear you'll need and which equipment is best suited to your particular fishing venture. You'll find out more about saltwater fish, how to catch them, and what to do with the catch you bring home. That includes delicious recipes you can use to turn your catch into a tasty meal! You'll also learn some tips and tricks and tried-and-true fishing methods. Whether you're a novice or a practiced fisherman, there's always room to grow. Perhaps most importantly, in this book you'll come to understand the ethical responsibilities of fishers and appreciate the part you can play in environmental stewardship. Are you ready to dive into the world of saltwater fishing? Let's get started!

# CHAPTER 1
# PREPARING TO FISH

# 8  SALTWATER FISHING LIKE A PRO

To have the best fishing experience, it's important to know some information before you go! Research all the city, state, and federal fishing laws where you live. You may need to obtain a fishing license or registration. If so, you'll need to bring documentation that you've obtained the proper licenses with you.

Know what fish species you're allowed to catch in your location and the season in which you're practicing. Know the size limits and number of fish you're allowed to catch.

This regulation chart shows the fishing bag and size limits for saltwater species.

It's also of the utmost importance that you take safety precautions before embarking on your fishing excursion. No matter your level of skill or expertise, accidents are always possible. Give yourself the best chance to avoid mishaps and return home safely.

## KNOW BEFORE YOU GO

Always check the weather forecast before going fishing. Wear appropriate clothing for the expected conditions. Take an extra set of dry clothes in a waterproof bag. In some areas you'll want to avoid red, yellow, or black clothing, which can attract gnats, black flies, and mosquitoes. Also, leave flip-flops at home. You'll need waders, wading shoes, or waterproof shoes or boots to remain stable for shore fishing or slippery boat decks.

Be ready for sun, wind, and water, as well as any sudden storms. Minimize the effects of a day in the sun by wearing a hat and sunglasses. Apply sunscreen, especially to your face. Be prepared for rain and thunderstorms, even if they are not in the forecast. Weather over the ocean changes quickly. If you need a rain jacket or windbreaker, wear one that fits loosely in the shoulders. That will give you room to handle your rod easily. Be sure to bring a well-stocked first-aid kit.

While boating, keep an eye on the sky. Watch for approaching thunderstorms. If your fishing rod buzzes, lightning may be about to strike. Crouch down and put your hands on your knees. If you see lightning or hear thunder, stop fishing. Immediately turn back to shore. Stay low in the boat. Regardless of the weather, never sit on the side of a boat or dangle your legs toward the water.

10 SALTWATER FISHING LIKE A PRO

This fisherman is wearing a hat, sunglasses, gloves, and a windbreaker. He's protected from the sun and ready for the elements!

# PREPARING TO FISH     11

## PRACTICE WATER SAFETY

If you use a boat, check wave height. Be sure the size of the boat is right for the conditions. The bigger the boat, the more stable it is in rough seas. The smaller the boat, the more likely you are to get seasick.

Seasickness, a type of motion sickness, can ruin a fishing trip. You might have nausea or feel tired or dizzy. You might sweat or get a headache. Worst of all, you might vomit. Children between the ages of 2 and 12, women, and the elderly are more likely to suffer from seasickness. To prevent seasickness, watch your diet before the trip. Avoid a big meal of greasy food, bread, or pasta. Instead, choose a light meal that includes fruits, vegetables, and plenty of water.

Feeling seasick isn't fun, but there are lots of things that can help! Eating ginger can settle your stomach. So can sipping on a carbonated drink.

On the boat, sit near the middle for the most stable ride. Some fishing boats have inside cabins. However, if you feel seasick, stay in the fresh air. Focus your vision on the horizon. Some over-the-counter and prescription drugs, taken with adult guidance, can prevent or reduce symptoms of seasickness. However, some medicines work only if taken before setting out to sea.

## OBEY SAFETY RULES

Follow boating safety rules. Before you leave, tell someone where you will be fishing and when you'll be back. Describe the boat. Ask your friend to call the U.S. Coast Guard if your return is long overdue.

Obey the requirements on the boat manufacturer's capacity plate. This plate tells the number of people and weight allowed on the boat. Balance the weight of people and gear evenly throughout the boat. Otherwise, the boat could capsize, or overturn.

Safe operation of a boat depends on the condition of the driver. According to the U.S. Coast Guard, alcohol use is involved in almost one-third of all recreational boating deaths. Boating under the influence of alcohol or other drugs is just as illegal as driving a car under the influence. The U.S. Coast Guard and all states define legal limits for alcohol use in their waters. They are comparable to limits for driving motor vehicles. Passengers under the influence also risk dangerous falls overboard. Never board a boat if the operator or any passenger has been using alcohol or other drugs. Discourage alcohol use while underway.

## FISHING REGULATIONS

Recreational fishing regulations vary from state to state. For example, saltwater fishing in Alaska is open year-round (with the exception of certain species). In New York, saltwater fishing season is only during the spring.

Since each state is different, it's up to you to do your own research before setting off to fish. You can keep up to date with your local saltwater fishing regulations by checking your state government website. Regulations are subject to change at any time, so it's important to check often in case the rules have been updated.

Many fisheries and species are threatened by commercial overfishing, overpopulation of one or more species, and poisons in the water. Knowing what you're allowed to catch and what's safe to eat is incredibly important. Don't put yourself at risk! And don't harm vulnerable species. You'll see that size limits and bag limits are sometimes seasonal and there are often different rules for finfish and shellfish.

Check your state calendars, fish charts, and regulations so you can know before you go. You can also download apps that notify you with updates regarding this information. Here's the information from a few of the states where saltwater fishing is most popular:

### Alaska
www.adfg.alaska.gov/index.cfm?adfg=fishregulations.sport

### Florida
myfwc.com/fishing/saltwater/recreational/
Download the "Fish Rules" app to keep up to date on state regulations.

*continued on next spread*

**Louisiana**
www.wlf.louisiana.gov/subhome/recreational-fishing

**Massachusetts**
www.mass.gov/service-details/recreational-saltwater-fishing-regulations

**New York**
www.dec.ny.gov/outdoor/7894.html

**North Carolina**
www.deq.nc.gov/about/divisions/marine-fisheries/rules-proclamations-and-size-and-bag-limits/recreational-size-and-bag-limits

**Texas**
tpwd.texas.gov/regulations/outdoor-annual/fishing/

**Virginia**
www.mrc.virginia.gov/recreational.shtm

## FISHING ETIQUETTE

With the popularity of sport fishing, anglers must often share the water. Fishing etiquette calls for respecting other anglers. Lend a hand if others ask for help. If another person loses an item in the water, help retrieve it if you can do so safely. Offer to tow a boat with a disabled motor. Give directions. Lend extra line or other equipment. Share knowledge of fishing techniques, habitat, or behavior with less experienced fishers who are eager to learn. Most important, render aid or call emergency services when needed.

Another important rule of good sportsmanship is to stay quiet. Loud voices, music, barking dogs, or other loud noises scare away fish and disturb others who are fishing. In addition, it is a courtesy to move on to another place if someone is already fishing a spot. If that's where you want to fish, come back later after the other angler leaves. If you are in a boat, stay away from anglers who are fishing from the shore. Also stay away from other boats already working an area, whether they are at anchor or moving as they fish.

If you are part of a fishing party aboard a boat, place your rod in a holder to save your spot. Never move another angler's rod from its holder without permission. In general, respect other anglers' property. Also respect property owners' rights if you must cross private land to get to the place where you want to fish.

Give fellow anglers a fair chance to catch fish. Don't crowd fishing buddies or strangers. Keep your fishing line clear of others' lines so that they don't get tangled. If someone hooks a fish, keep your own line out of the way so that the angler can bring in the catch.

Always look behind you and to both sides before casting so that you don't endanger others. You don't want your hook to injure someone's eye or skin. Never cast toward another person or over their head. If you or another angler gets a hook caught in their skin, there is an appropriate way to take it out. Carefully push the point of the hook forward through the skin. Cut off the barb on the end. Then pull the rest of the hook back through, the way it came in.

Fishing boat operators should quickly launch and pull their boats out of the water. Move away from the boat ramp to load and unload food, drink, and fishing gear so that others don't have to wait to use the ramp.

## PROTECT YOURSELF

The ocean poses dangers, even close to shore. Always go fishing with someone else. If an emergency occurs, your buddy can rescue you or call for help.

The first rule for shore fishing is to never turn your back on the ocean. A sudden high wave can knock you off your footing. The impact can also cause head, neck, or spine injuries similar to the whiplash experienced in a rear-end car accident. To some, facing the ocean is also a way to show respect for its awesome power.

If you spend time around water, knowing how to swim is important. Even if you can swim, you still need water safety and rescue skills appropriate for fishing and boating.

You always need a personal flotation device when fishing from a boat. Many people who have drowned in boating accidents might have lived if they had worn life jackets. Choose one approved by the U.S. Coast Guard and be sure it fits correctly.

Also, be sure to bring at least two forms of communication with you when boating. Then you can contact someone if you are in trouble and get help much more quickly. Useful items include a cell phone, hand-held waterproof radio, personal emergency locator beacon, and red flares. A sound signal, such as a horn, can also be helpful.

If your buddy falls into the water, resist the urge to jump in after them unless you are a certified lifeguard. Instead, extend a pole or rope, or toss a life preserver or boat cushion. The American Red Cross and other groups include such skills in their lesson programs.

PREPARING TO FISH    17

A life jacket like those pictured here could save your life! Even skilled swimmers need life jackets.

## NAVIGATING THE WATER

The Coast Guard and the U.S. Army Corps of Engineers install and maintain a system of buoys (also called channel markers) to help boaters safely navigate federal waters. All boats use the system to help sea traffic run smoothly.

Knowing the colors and shapes of the various buoys helps boat operators follow the rules and take the correct course in the water. This helps prevent collisions and other trouble. For example, large boats operating near coastlines risk running aground or getting stuck in the sand if they enter water that is too shallow. Reefs, underwater wrecks, and other hazards also pose dangers to fishing boats.

Be sure to follow all water traffic rules. Pay attention to signs and buoys.

Buoys tell boat operators which part of a waterway to use, depending on where they are headed. Some buoys have a light on top. That way boaters can see them at night or in fog. A saying familiar to sailors is "Red, right, returning." That means if you are coming into a harbor, keep the red buoys on your right. When you are leaving the harbor, keep the green ones on your right. A cylinder-shaped buoy with a cone-like top is called a nun. A cylinder-shaped buoy with a flat top is called a can.

Additional colors and shapes of buoys indicate such information as safe water and locations of pipelines, fish trap areas, and other features. Buoys are marked on nautical charts, which all boating anglers need on board.

Obey no-wake zones, speed limits, and rules about areas where you can and cannot operate a boat. Wake is the path of waves created by the movement of the boat. Signs that say "No Wake" mean you should slow down to protect property, docked boats, or wildlife from damage from big waves. Also slow your speed in foul weather and around smaller boats so that you don't rock them with your wake.

# CHAPTER 2
# GRAB YOUR GEAR!

The gear you'll need depends on where you plan to do your fishing and what kind of fish you're hoping to catch. Generally speaking, saltwater fish are bigger and stronger than freshwater fish. Thus, saltwater fishing gear needs to be stronger to contend with these fish.

## CHOOSE A ROD AND REEL

It's easy to recognize a saltwater rod. There are two places to hold it. Hold the grip above the reel to set the hook. Use the grip below the reel to support the rod as you land the fish. Compare rods according to length, weight, and flexibility. Long rods cast farthest, but you need more physical strength to cast them than shorter ones. Shorter rods are easier to handle and store. If you're a beginner, start with

Don't use freshwater gear for saltwater fishing. You need salt-resistant gear with the proper grips to land your fish.

a spinning rod that measures 6 to 7 feet (1.8 to 2.1 meters) long; it will work for most saltwater species. You can add new rods as your needs and experience change.

Reels hold, release, and roll up fishing line. Revolving-spool reels roll to unwind line. They can handle heavy line, but they are subject to backlash. Backlash is tangled line that occurs when the line is reeled out too quickly. Fixed-spool reels let out line from a stationary spool. They are less likely to tangle the line. Not every reel works with every rod. You need to match your reel to your rod. The best bet is a rod and reel packaged together by the manufacturer.

## BUILT FOR THE TASK

You don't know which fish might head your way, so buy a variety of hooks. Match the size of the hook to the size of your bait and the kind of fish you are trying to catch. For natural bait, use a circle hook or a J hook. A circle hook will not catch in a fish's stomach. If a fish swallows it, it rolls back into the mouth and catches there. A circle hook is also easy to remove. A J hook is commonly used as well, but a fish can swallow this hook and it can be hard to remove. Some artificial baits, called lures, use treble hooks. A treble hook is one with three hooks on the same stem. You have a better chance of catching a fish with this hook. But be careful not to hook yourself while working with one.

Choose line that is built for the task of reeling in the size fish you want. Line is rated according to strength. Breaking strength is the number of pounds or kilograms of weight the line can hold without breaking. A 20-pound (9.1 kg) test line, for example, can hold 20 pounds (9.1 kg) without breaking. Thickness helps determine strength. Thick line is usually stronger than thin line. However, thinner line can be harder for fish to see. Some kinds of fish, such as bream, will not bite if they see the line. These fish are said to be line shy.

Monofilament line is the most popular type of fishing line. Made from a single strand of nylon, it is good for casting. It comes in a wide selection of strengths, from 1-pound (0.45 kg) weight to more than 200-pound (90.7 kg) weight. Braided line has several strands of fiber. It is best for reef fishing because corals can fray single-strand line. Line for deepwater trolling is made from wire.

You also need sinkers, swivels, and snaps. Sinkers are metal weights that keep the hook and bait from floating on the surface. Swivels and snaps tie to the end of the line. Swivels prevent twisted line. Snaps make changing hooks easy.

This saltwater rod and line is strong enough to land big game.

GRAB YOUR GEAR! 25

## HOW TO CHOOSE

When you're starting out, it can be overwhelming to discover just how many choices there are when it comes to gear. There are several different rods and lines made of various materials. How can you narrow down the choices? In this section we'll take a closer look at rods and lines and the materials used to make them. This rough breakdown will help you decide which type of rod and line will be best for the kind of fishing you're hoping to do.

### CARBON FIBER ROD
Best for: long casts
Pros: stronger than graphite
Cons: Heavier to use

### FIBERGLASS ROD
Best for: trolling rods; fighting large, heavy fish
Pros: flexible and strong
Cons: slower response time

### GRAPHITE ROD
Best for: light biters, deep-water fish
Pros: sensitive
Cons: less flexible than fiberglass

We'll also help you choose the best saltwater fishing lines:

### MONOFILAMENT LINE
Best for: most types of fishing
Pros: thin, strong, water-resistant, stretchy
Cons: will break down under sunlight, needs to be changed every six months

*continued on next spread*

## BRAIDED LINE

Best for: bottom fishing
Pros: casts farther and faster; long-lasting, doesn't break down in the sunlight
Cons: doesn't stretch, not good for trolling

## FLOUROCARBON LINE

Best for: tying leaders to saltwater fishing lines
Pros: almost invisible underwater
Cons: very stiff, breaks down easily

## WIRE

Best for: trolling
Pros: good for catching toothy fish
Cons: may break

Which type of rod and line do you think would be best for catching this marlin?

## CHOOSE YOUR BAIT

Natural baits are usually just called bait, while artificial baits are called lures. Many saltwater anglers—and the game fish they are seeking—prefer natural bait. But lures can catch lots of fish too.

Live small fish are popular bait. Use pilchards to catch snappers and other small-to-medium-size fish. Pinfish are somewhat bigger and tempt larger fish. Use small mullets, called finger mullets, for small sport fish. You can use 2-pounders (0.9 kg) for big game fish.

Another popular bait is menhaden, a marine fish also known as shad, pogy, or bunker. Recreational anglers use it while bottom fishing to attract such fish as striped bass, weakfish, and mackerel. Saltwater anglers also use shrimp, crab, and even worms.

Chum is natural bait made of fish that is ground like hamburger. Chum is held in a net bag or wire cage and dragged behind a boat to attract fish to the area. Blood and fish oil from the chum create a slick on the water. Chum is not bait in the sense of being dangled from a hook. You still need a hook with bait or a lure.

You can buy natural bait in bait shops or tackle stores. You can also catch it yourself with a cast net or sabiki rig. A cast net has weighted edges. Throw it so that it spreads across the surface and sinks. With luck, it will be full of baitfish when you pull it in. A sabiki rig attaches to line on a sabiki rod and reel. The rig has six hooks, each with a small, colorful bead. Often, the beads are neon pink or green.

These shrimp will be used as live bait for saltwater fishing.

## LURE YOUR FISH

Game fish are attracted to motion, shapes, colors, smells, and even sounds. Lures appeal to these senses. Lures are artificial baits with hooks attached. They are made from such materials as wood, metal, plastic, glass, fur, feathers, and rubber. Some examples of lures include flies, spoons, spinners, plugs, poppers, and soft baits.

Saltwater flies are lightweight lures tied to hooks to attract fish. They are designed to look like small fish, crustaceans, insects, and other marine animals as they move through the water. Use them with a fly rod and heavy line. Some flies land softly on the surface, and others are designed to move underwater.

## GRAB YOUR GEAR! 29

These saltwater lures are made to attract tuna and marlin.

Metal lures called spoons and spinners attract fish with movement and reflection. The silver or gold spoons and spinner blades reflect sunlight, which attracts fish. Spoons usually have oval shapes. They wobble through water. Spinners spin. They have blades that rotate in circles.

A plug is a wooden or plastic lure shaped and painted to look like a small fish. Manufactured plugs are engineered, painted, and tested to imitate small baitfish. Some plugs, called poppers, make a loud popping or buzzing sound. They attract game fish with noise. Saltwater plugs are easy to lose or wear out. Fish that break your line can steal your plugs. Also, salt water ruins paint and rusts hooks.

Soft baits are soft, flexible plastic lures. They look like shrimp, crabs, small fish, or worms. Some manufacturers

## CARING FOR YOUR GEAR

Store sharp items such as hooks, lures, gaffs, and knives when they are not in use. On shore, keep small items in a tackle box. On a boat, choose places where a sudden tip of the boat won't send them flying. Store hooks and lures in a closed tackle box. Always keep your rod in a holder or locker so that no one will trip over it.

After fishing, clean your equipment to prevent saltwater damage. Rinse your rod and reel with fresh water. When the season ends, separate the rod and reel. Soak the rod in soapy water and remove any salt deposits with a soft brush.

At the end of the season, you'll need to throw away about 75 percent of the line from the reel. Rinse the reel in fresh water and let it dry. Follow the manufacturer's directions to clean and lubricate all moving parts. Add new line. Store in a padded container in a cool, dry place.

add fishy scents to soft bait to appeal to a game fish's strong sense of smell. Store soft baits away from other lures. The chemicals used to make them can ruin hard plastic lures and paint finishes.

## LAND THAT FISH!

Gear for landing a fish or getting it into a boat includes leaders, landing nets, and gaffs. A leader is a wire or monofilament line that connects fishing line to the hook. The leader is heavier than the line in order to handle the weight of the fish. For example, you might pair a 20-pound (9.1 kg) test line with a 100-pound (45.4 kg) test leader.

Landing nets let you scoop fish from the water. Nets are made of twine, nylon, rubber, monofilament net, or neoprene. Neoprene is a synthetic rubber that causes the least harm to fish. A gaff is a big hook. Use it to grasp a heavy fish and lift it into the boat.

A few more basics are all you need. Take a toenail clipper to cut line. A pair of rustproof needle-nose pliers come in handy for unhooking fish and other tasks. You also need an assortment of knives.

## HELPFUL GADGETS

Some great gadgets can help you catch fish. Depth finders, fish finders, and global positioning systems (GPS) are items you might want to try.

Depth finders are navigational instruments. They use either radar or sound waves to tell how deep water is. Some models show pictures of the ocean floor. A fish finder uses radar to determine the location of fish and the depth at which they are swimming. Some fish finders measure surface temperature. Others include speed sensors. You can

32　SALTWATER FISHING LIKE A PRO

Always have a net ready to help you land your catch!

also choose LCD or color screens. Color screens have better images, but they are more expensive. A global positioning system (GPS) uses satellites to pinpoint places on Earth. It tells boaters where they are located. It also helps them return to favorite fishing spots.

While electronic gadgets are fun to have and use, some cost a lot of money. Watch your budget. You may get more pleasure—and catch more fish—by investing in a better quality rod and reel. Remember, people have been catching fish for thousands of years. Fishermen were successful even without these high-tech gadgets.

There are many different methods of saltwater fishing. The type of method you'll employ will depend on what kind of fish you're hoping to reel in. Discover which fishing techniques were developed to catch which saltwater species.

## TYPES OF SALTWATER FISHING

Some popular types of saltwater fishing include bottom fishing, trolling, structure fishing, jetty fishing, float fishing, surf fishing, jigging, still fishing, fly fishing, and spear fishing.

Bottom fishing is one of the most popular fishing techniques in salt water. With this method, the hook is suspended one or two feet (0.3 or 0.6 m) from the ocean floor. You can bottom fish from a dock, pier, beach, or surf. You can also use this method from a boat, especially near coral, artificial reefs, or underwater structures like sunken ships.

Trolling is another common fishing method in salt water, especially in the open ocean. The fisher puts bait or a lure in the water and drags it behind a powerboat. Use trolling for billfish, sailfish, tuna, and marlin. You can also use it closer to shore for kingfish, bluefish, and jacks. Some anglers use chum to attract fish to their boats when trolling. Drift fishing is similar to trolling, except that you "go with the flow" without a powered motor.

Structure fishing is popular for fishing from piers, docks, bridges, and other structures. The most commonly fished structure is a jetty. A jetty is a barrier made of rocks, concrete, wood, or rubble that sticks out into a body of water. To fish, you walk the length of the jetty. They can be uneven and slippery, so you need safety footwear called jetty creepers.

START FISHING! 37

This photo shows the trolling method. The lures are being dragged behind a powerboat.

# 38 SALTWATER FISHING LIKE A PRO

This boy is fishing off the side of a jetty.

Float fishing is a method that uses a bobber or other floating device. The device stays on top of the water. A sinker attached to the line keeps the bait underwater. The float controls the depth of the hook. When the bobber dips underwater, you have likely hooked a fish.

Surf fishing is done from a beach or by wading out from shore. Fresh bait is preferred, but you can use metal lures, especially plugs. Some popular surf fishing targets include striped bass, bluefish, weakfish, red drum, and snook.

In still fishing, you keep bait in the water as you fish from a pier, bridge, or anchored boat. Still fishing is a good way to catch giant sea bass, rockfish, and barracuda. If you are using a lure, try jigging. Drop in the lure, then jerk it back to the surface. The movement gets the attention of such fish as grunts and black sea bass.

Fly fishing uses a rod to cast lightweight flies on heavy line. You hold the line across your palm and fingers instead of on a reel. Fly fishing is among the least common types of fishing in salt water, but its popularity is growing. Fly fishing usually occurs close to shore. However, such species as sailfish, marlin, and Pacific bluefish have been caught in the open ocean with fly fishing gear.

## FISHING WITH A SPEARGUN

Spear fishing is an underwater sport that uses a speargun instead of a rod and reel. A speargun is used to fire a spear that strikes the fish.

The fisher can hunt by free diving, snorkeling, or scuba diving. Free diving is simply holding your breath under water. Snorkeling is swimming using swim fins and a diving mask equipped with a breathing tube. "Scuba" stands for "self-contained underwater breathing apparatus." In this form of diving, a container of compressed air allows you to stay underwater for longer periods of time and reach greater depths.

You can fish by diving from the shore or from a boat. When boats are present, use a buoy tied to the speargun to warn others that you are underwater. Spear fishing is particularly popular in Hawaii. It is legal in most states. However, in many areas, you are restricted to hunting certain species. There are also regulations about the type of power the speargun uses. Spear guns are dangerous weapons. Never shoot one toward another person, dock, campsite, or boat ramp.

This fisherman wears a wetsuit and scuba gear. He's holding a speargun.

## SPEARGUN SAFETY

Spearguns are very dangerous. They should only be used by licensed adults. There are strict rules about where and when these weapons are allowed to be used. Many of the rules concerning the safe use and handling of firearms, or guns, can also be applied to spearguns. Here are some of the basics:

### DON'T
- Don't load a speargun out of the water. That's because spearguns need the resistance of the water to be loaded properly.
- Don't fire a speargun out of water. Underwater, a speargun can shoot 20 feet. Out of water, it can shoot 200 feet.
- Don't point a speargun at anything you do not want to kill. Spearguns should only ever be pointed at fish targets. Otherwise, a deadly accident could happen.
- Don't rely on the speargun safety. Never assume that your speargun is safe because the safety is on. Accidents can happen this way.

### DO
- Do keep your finger away from the trigger until you are ready to shoot. Triggers can be pressed accidentally. If you keep your finger away from the trigger, you keep everyone safer.
- Do know what is behind your target. There may be other fishers in the water around you. Don't put them at risk by shooting anywhere near them.
- Do make sure there are no tangles in your rigging.
- Do take care of your speargun. Rinse it with fresh water after each use and make sure to dry it completely. This will help you avoid rust.
- Do replace any parts that need to be replaced seasonally.

## FIND THE BEST TIME

The best time to fish depends on the type of fish you seek and their habits and habitat. Off the South Carolina coast, for example, spring and fall are the best times for fishing. Food for game fish is plentiful then.

Many game fish eat young fish called fry. For example, halibut and calico bass like to eat Pacific surfperch fry. Both sport fishes usually swim in deeper water. However, they will come closer to shore when the surfperch grow to about two inches (5 cm) long. Along America's West Coast, that happens between March and July. That's a good time to fish for halibut and calico bass in the Pacific.

If you are surf fishing, you'll have better luck in the early morning or late evening when the tide is coming in or going out. The water currents carry the shrimp, small crabs, and baitfish that bigger fish eat. These baitfish have difficulty controlling their movement in strong currents, so they are easier for bigger fish to feed on. Start fishing an hour or two before each change in tide and continue for up to an hour afterward. For boat fishing at these times of day, drop your bait near the tide line. The tide line is the front edge of the moving water, whichever direction it flows.

Pier fishing is best at night. Small fish swim in toward the lights, and larger fish soon follow. For sharks, you'll have better luck fishing after the sun goes down. They are more active at night. In fact, most species, including snapper, feed at night. You can fish for many species during the first five hours after sundown. Be sure you have flashlights so that you can see what you're doing! Successful night fishing often depends on attracting fish to movement or smell. Chumming is a good method to use when night fishing by boat.

## START FISHING! 43

This father and son are surf fishing at sunset.

## BIRDS AND BAIT

Use the two Bs to look for fish: bait and birds. You can usually find fish near one or both. Drop your line where your prey finds its favorite food. Also, watch for seabirds. They often eat the same foods that fish like. If you see birds, sport fish may be feeding in the same area. Birds may hover over an area or peck in wet sand. In southern California, for example, birds called sandpipers eat sand crabs. So do such fish as corbina and barred surfperch. If you see the birds digging, you are likely to find the fish in nearby water.

Sometimes, you can find game fish by scanning the surface for light reflecting off fins or tails. Fish on the move may break the surface or disturb it. Watch for moving water in the shape of a V. Or look for a series of ripples (called nervous water) moving on the surface.

## MAIN LOCATIONS

You can use most fishing methods in each of the three main locations for saltwater fishing: shore, inshore, and offshore. Shore fishing includes fishing from a beach, pier, jetty, rock formation, or another coastal feature. Inshore fishing occurs within sight of the coastline. It includes fishing in relatively shallow water in a bay that leads to the open ocean. Offshore fishing, or deep-sea fishing, occurs in the open ocean. This is the place to go for big sport fish. When going offshore, many anglers take a party boat for drift fishing or a charter boat that offers drift fishing along with trolling and bottom fishing.

You'll find fish where they hide or hunt. The more you know about fish behavior and habitats, the easier it

START FISHING! 45

These people are enjoying saltwater fishing off a pier in Florida.

will be to find the best places to drop or cast your line. Knowing coastal features and the composition of the ocean floor in your area will help you know where to fish. If you find the game fish's food, the larger fish you are seeking are likely lurking nearby.

Some fish hide in stands of kelp, near coral reefs, or in shipwrecks. For instance, you'll find grouper and snapper near coral reefs, waiting for prey to swim by. That's where you'll want to drop your bait. Other fish chase their food. Some small fish hide under piers and eat organisms that attach themselves to the structure. Game fish swim under

Coral reefs are harmed by overfishing and pollution. By doing your part to protect coral reefs, you can help the many marine species that they support.

the pier looking for a good meal. At sea, look for strong ocean currents, which carry small fish and shrimp. That's where to look for larger fish that eat these species.

Learn about habitats of baitfish and other marine organisms such as crabs, mussels, and clam worms. For example, in northeastern states, bluefish, striped bass, and bonito usually swim too far from shore for surf fishing. However, you can catch them from the beach when sand eels are around. (Sand eels favor shorelines with soft sand or mud bottoms.)

Water temperature also affects where different species swim. Shallow water is usually warmer than deep water. Water closer to the surface is warmer than deeper water in the same place. Also consider the season and latitude where you are fishing. Latitude is the distance north or south of the equator. Fish in warmer waters for sailfish, marlin, and tiger sharks. Fish in cold water for cod and Atlantic mackerel.

# CHAPTER 4
# MAKE YOUR CATCH

It's important to have a plan for what you'd like to do with your fish once you've caught it. Some fishers prefer to catch and release. Others enjoy bringing home an impressive catch and turning it into a delicious meal. This is a major decision which shouldn't be taken lightly. Make sure you know before you go!

## KNOW YOUR LIMIT

No matter when or where you fish, you will not want to harvest every fish you catch. The fish you catch may be too small or the species may be spawning, endangered, or out of season. Perhaps you've already caught the legal limit for the day. In some cases, regulations require release of certain species. In Florida, for example, anglers cannot keep goliath or Nassau grouper. The harvesting of snook, red drum, and spotted sea trout is limited to certain sizes and times of the year. These kinds of conservation efforts have restored or sustained some fish species in Florida and other states.

## LET IT GO

Catching fish and letting them go is called catch-and-release fishing. Some anglers enjoy the challenge of catching fish but release all the fish they catch. Others practice catch-and-release fishing only in certain circumstances. Critics of the practice say being caught and released—only to be hooked again—is cruel to fish. However, it is one way to ensure that some fish grow to adulthood and reproduce. That means more fish for future anglers.

If you are going to release a fish, do your best to ensure its survival. Use equipment and methods to protect the fish. For instance, use circle hooks or hooks without barbs for catch-and-release fishing.

## MAKE YOUR CATCH 51

Do your part to protect marine ecosystems. Never fish beyond your limit. Always release vulnerable species.

52 SALTWATER FISHING LIKE A PRO

Watching a catch swim away unharmed can be very satisfying!

The two main reasons a released fish dies are stress and injury. Physical stress from fighting disrupts a fish's metabolism. Metabolism refers to the body's chemical processes. If you release the fish right away, the imbalance soon returns to normal. However, a long fight can exhaust a fish. It may not recover. To keep stress to a minimum, use tackle strong enough to reel in the fish as quickly as possible. Decide whether to keep or release a hooked fish before taking it out of the water.

## PRACTICE VENTING

Bringing a fish from deep to shallow water too quickly stresses it. This can happen with reef fishing. Excess gas collects in the fish's body. A fish in trouble has bulging eyes or a bloated belly. Sometimes, its stomach sticks out of its mouth. Before letting the fish go, release the excess gas. Venting is the way to do that.

Since 2008, federal regulations have required that anglers carry a venting tool when fishing reefs in the Gulf of Mexico. For venting, a fisher can use a 16-gauge needle stuck in a block of wood or a syringe without the plunger. One can also use a manufactured venting tool. (Never use a knife or an ice pick.)

Place the point of the venting tool under a scale, about 2 inches (5 cm) behind the base of a pectoral fin. Pectoral fins lie just behind the gill openings. Gills are breathing organs. They are found on each side of the fish, just behind the head. Gently insert the needle a short way into the body cavity. Gases will escape. Then you can safely release the fish. Never puncture an inverted stomach or shove it back into the fish's mouth. The stomach will go back where it belongs once you release the fish.

## GENTLE HANDLING

Prevent harm to the fish from the hook or improper handling. If possible, remove the hook while the fish is still in the water. If the fish has swallowed the hook, leave the hook alone. Snip the line as close to the hook as possible. Over time, most hooks dissolve. The fish will survive. Avoid stainless-steel hooks. They won't dissolve and are outlawed in some areas.

If you intend to release a fish, do not lift it directly from the water to the boat. Instead, use a landing net. Never gaff a fish you intend to release unless you can gaff it through the lower jaw. If you must handle a fish, use wet hands and support the fish horizontally.

Don't touch its gills or eyes, and don't hold it by the jaw. It could lose its ability to feed—and then starve. Gently release the fish headfirst.

## PREPARING YOUR CATCH

Fish is low in calories, high in protein, and low in saturated fat. Fish oil is a good source of omega-3 fatty acids, especially from saltwater species such as tuna, herring, and mackerel. Omega-3 fatty acids are important for children's growth and development. They also lower the risk of heart disease and other ailments.

If you plan to eat your catch, keep the fish cold and clean it as soon as possible. If you can't clean it immediately after catching it, keep it cold and wet until you can. Another option is to keep the fish alive in a live well or a basket kept in the water. Observe fish cleaning rules and regulations for the area. Some places ban fish cleaning on boats or beaches. Many marinas and boat-launch areas have fish cleaning stations for anglers to use.

## MAKE YOUR CATCH 55

### RECORD YOUR CATCH!

Whether you choose to eat or release your catch, you might want to record the event. You can keep the memory with a photograph, video, or fiberglass model.

For a photograph, choose a background without buckets, coolers, and other gear. Take off sunglasses and hats that cast shadows on your face. Keep the fish wet. It will show up better. Hold it by supporting it horizontally.

Camcorders, cell phone cameras, and other video equipment can also help you remember your fishing trip. For underwater activities like speargun fishing, use a waterproof camcorder case, an underwater camcorder, or a high-definition recorder.

A taxidermist is a person who mounts fish and other animals for display. Today, taxidermists may design fiberglass models. If you'd like to mount a fish this way, take several color pictures. Weigh it and carefully measure its dimensions. Make careful notes about outstanding characteristics. Your model will look like the real thing.

Fishing with a buddy keeps you safe. It also means you'll have help photographing your best catch!

You will need a scaling knife, pocketknife, and fillet knife for cleaning fish. Be sure to get an adult's permission and supervision before using these tools. A scaling knife has a dull blade. It removes scales when you clean your catch. Use a pocketknife or other sharp knife with a relatively short blade to remove a fish's internal organs. A fillet knife has a long, narrow, flexible blade. Use it to separate flesh from bone.

There are two main methods of cleaning fish: gutting them (removing the scales and internal organs) and filleting them. Filleting separates the flesh from the bones and sometimes the skin.

If the fish has scales, use a scaling knife to remove them. Lay the fish on its side, perpendicular to your body. Hold it by the tail. Place the knife edge against the tail end of the fish at a 45-degree angle (about half of a square corner). Face the blade toward you. Stroke the blade away from you toward the head. Move the blade against the direction of the scales. Scaling is a messy job. Do it outside if you can. If inside, keep the fish in a tub or sink full of water while you scale it.

To gut a fish, use a pocketknife or another sharp knife with a short blade. Lay the fish on its side or back. Insert the knife, with the blade facing out, at the end of the fish. Pull the blade through the belly skin and toward the head, all the way to the gills. Remove the internal organs and gills, including any small bones. Leave the fins in place. You can easily remove them after cooking. If you want to remove the head, cut just behind the pectoral fins, from the top down.

To fillet a fish, use a fillet knife. Slice the length of the fish's back down to the backbone. Leaving the rib cage intact, follow the curve of the rib cage with the blade. If

MAKE YOUR CATCH  57

This woman is cleaning the scales off a fish using a scaling knife.

you want to remove the skin, use a sawing motion. Trim any excess fat.

After cleaning fish, chill immediately to keep fish fresh. Use a cooler of ice or put fish in a slurry. A slurry is a thin mixture of water and other material. Try mixing seawater with saltwater ice. The salt makes the water-and-ice mixture colder than ice made with fresh water.

This fisherman is cleaning and filleting saltwater fish aboard his deep-sea fishing boat.

## GET COOKING!

For many anglers, the best part of a fishing trip is the old-fashioned fish fry that follows. Frying is a popular method for cooking fish. Dip the fish in a mixture of milk and beaten eggs. Then drag it through bread crumbs. Fry it in vegetable oil in a frying pan or deep fryer. It tastes good! However, frying is not the healthiest way to cook fish. Frying increases the fish's fat and calorie content. For a healthier meal, grill or broil fish so that the fat drips away from the flesh.

The best time to cook fish is right after it is caught. The second-best time is within a few hours. Freeze what you can't cook and eat that soon. To save fish for another occasion, tightly wrap the gutted fish in plastic wrap. Then cover with heavy aluminum foil, tape the package shut, and freeze. Place fish fillets in a resealable freezer bag. Cover the fillets with fresh water. Carefully press out any air and seal the bag. Label with the type of fish and the date before placing the bag in the freezer. Frozen fish keep for up to two months.

Keep your fish on ice until you can cook it.

## RECIPES TO TRY

### GRILLED SARDINES

## INGREDIENTS

- 8 medium whole fresh sardines (about 1 pound total), gutted, rinsed inside and out, and patted dry
- 1 tablespoon plus 1 ½ teaspoons extra-virgin olive oil
- ¾ teaspoon coarse salt
- ¼ teaspoon freshly ground pepper
- 6-inch baguette (about 4 ounces), cut diagonally into 16 thin slices
- 1 garlic clove, peeled
- vegetable-oil cooking spray
- 1 lemon, cut into wedges, for serving

## DIRECTIONS

1. Brush both sides of fish using 1 tablespoon oil. Season with 1/2 teaspoon salt and 1/8 teaspoon pepper.
2. Rub cut sides of bread with garlic. Brush with remaining oil, and sprinkle with remaining salt and pepper.
3. Heat a grill pan over medium-high heat. Coat with cooking spray. Grill bread until crisp, about 1 minute per side. Grill sardines until cooked through, about 2 minutes per side. Serve on a platter with bread and lemon wedges.

## OVEN-BAKED SEA TROUT

### INGREDIENTS

- 2 pounds of sea trout fillets or other firm-fleshed fish
- 2 tablespoons minced onion
- ¼ cup stick unsalted butter, melted
- 2 tablespoons fresh lemon juice
- 1 teaspoon salt
- 1 teaspoon paprika
- 2 teaspoons red pepper flakes
- dash black pepper
- 1 tablespoon capers rinsed (optional)

### DIRECTIONS

1. Heat oven to 350°F.
2. Butter a glass casserole dish large enough so that the fillets aren't crowded.
3. Lay the fillets in a single layer in the glass casserole.
4. Whisk the melted butter, lemon juice, minced onion, salt, paprika, red pepper flakes, black pepper until well blended. (Also add the capers if you wish.) Pour the sauce evenly over the fillets.
5. Bake in the heated oven for 20 to 25 minutes. The fillets will be firm but still moist.
6. Serve immediately and spoon some additional sauce over the fillets.

# CHAPTER 5
# FISH RESPONSIBLY

Marine ecosystems are at risk. Overfishing, pollution, and habitat destruction have taken a large toll on saltwater species. It's essential to the future of the sport and the oceans that saltwater fishermen do their part to protect marine environments and animals. You can help!

## SAVE THE FISH!

Efforts are underway to protect the Atlantic bluefin tuna under the U.S. Endangered Species Act. According to the Center for Biological Diversity, overfishing of the tuna has caused an 80 percent decline in its population from what would be expected without fishing. Sport anglers have been responsible for catching thousands of tons of these fish. The species is popular for sushi and other dishes, so sport anglers may have sold their catches. Usually, commercial fishers sell tuna. In fact, most sport anglers consider selling the fish unethical.

The decline of many marine species is extremely worrying. Environmental organizations and the National Marine Fisheries Service have made efforts to attempt to sustain and restore at-risk species.

Sometimes, groups encourage taking a specific species. In 2010, an invasion of lionfish threatened coral reef fisheries along the East Coast, Florida Keys, and Gulf of Mexico. According to NOAA, the number of lionfish grew by 700 percent between 2004 and 2008. Lionfish eat many colorful fish that populate coral reefs. For example, they eat parrotfish, which eat algae on the reefs and keep the reefs clean. Reduced reef fish populations also include juvenile snapper and grouper sport fish. These effects can, in turn, reduce the number of tourists who come to fish, snorkel, and scuba dive in these areas. A reduction in tourism affects the economy in a negative way.

Humans may be the only predator that can stop the lionfish explosion. Lionfish are eaten as a delicacy in the Far East. So, conservationists in the United States are working with restaurant chefs to create recipes for lionfish. They hope this action will encourage catching, cooking, and eating the species. If the plan works, the number of lionfish will decrease. Then the coral reefs, and the variety of life among them, can be restored, sustained, or increased.

Efforts to curb bluefin tuna fishing can help save this species from dying out completely.

## SAVE SALTWATER HABITATS

Along with protecting fish, conservationists seek to protect saltwater fishing areas. In central California, for example, all human activity is banned in designated marine protected areas. The areas, most of which cover less than 1.5 square miles (3.9 sq km), are like state and national parks. The idea is to give these parts of the ocean a rest so that the water, plants, and animals can recover and thrive. The effort has had positive results. Fish in these reserves grow larger and produce more offspring than those in unprotected parts of the ocean.

Fitzgerald Marine Reserve in California is a designated marine protected area.

Oil spills and other types of severe pollution are extremely damaging to marine species and oceans. Oil is hazardous to fish. Unfortunately, thousands of oil spills happen in United States waters every year. The consequences can affect marine ecosystems for many years after the incident itself. Some worry that the dispersants—chemicals used to break up and scatter oil—are just as harmful as the oil itself!

In October 2021, a large oil spill released about 25,000 gallons of oil into the Pacific Ocean. The leak was caused by a crack in an oil pipeline underneath the ocean floor. The U.S. Coast Guard teamed up with the California Department of Fish and Wildlife and many others to clean up the spill as quickly as possible. The cleanup project took over three months to complete, but some damage was irreversible.

This team of environmental workers is helping clean up Huntington Beach, California, after the oil spill in 2021.

## FISHING REGULATIONS

Federal, state, and local governments hope to manage fisheries to ensure that there will always be plenty of fish. They address these kinds of issues with laws, regulations, and license requirements. Federal waters extend 200 miles (321.9 km) from the three-mile (4.8 km) limit where state waters end. In 2006, the Magnuson-Stevens Act created registration requirements for saltwater anglers. Federal regulators are creating a database to better track the number of people fishing and how much fishing they are doing.

    A list of regulations and rules can be found on the National Oceanic and Atmospheric Administration website. Regulations are broken down by region: Alaska, Atlantic Highly Migratory Species, Caribbean, Gulf of Mexico, New England/Mid Atlantic, Pacific Islands, South Atlantic, West

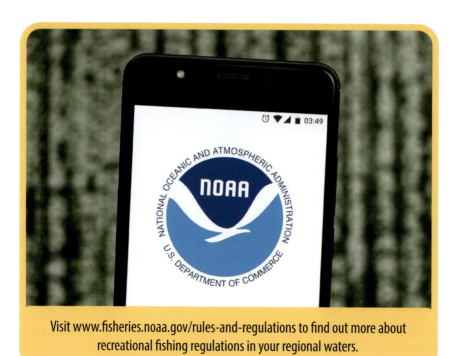

Visit www.fisheries.noaa.gov/rules-and-regulations to find out more about recreational fishing regulations in your regional waters.

## TOXINS IN FISH

Most saltwater fish contain traces of methylmercury. Methylmercury is a compound of mercury and carbon that is dangerous to living things. It accumulates in living organisms instead of being released as waste. Some fish contain high levels of this compound. Large fish and fish that have lived a long time have the most. Other contaminants in saltwater fish include pesticides and industrial waste. In fish, contaminants concentrate in the skin and fat.

Cooking cannot remove toxins. You can avoid problems by varying your sources of protein. Eat different kinds of fish during a given week or month. Check with your local health department or fishing authorities to learn which species in your area to limit or avoid. Young children and pregnant women are more sensitive to contaminants than others, so they should stick to low-risk fish. Fortunately, kid favorites like fish sticks and restaurant fish sandwiches are usually made from low-risk species.

Coast. These notices and rules are frequently updated. It's important to check the regulations for your regional waters often to remain up to date on the latest information.

State governments also manage saltwater resources in many coastal areas. States can determine the size and number of species that you can harvest. They impose fishing seasons by species. These seasons protect fish during the periods that they spawn, hatch, and grow to adulthood. They also govern gear and fishing methods by species.

Regulations vary by state. For instance, some states require fishing licenses for saltwater fishing, while other states do not. Some states set a minimum age for operating watercraft. Some require an approved boating education course. State regulations usually come from state agencies that deal with conservation, natural resources, fish, or wildlife. Look for rules for your area by contacting the appropriate agency. Do an internet search for "fishing regulations" and the state where you want to fish.

## YOU CAN HELP!

You can help care for beaches, oceans, and fisheries. First, leave the beach cleaner than you found it. Pick up litter left by others as well as your own trash. Carry out everything you brought to the beach, especially used fishing line and old or broken tackle. However, never remove seaweed, driftwood, or other natural items that provide food, habitat, or shelter for animals that live there. Stick to paths and walkways when walking near sand dunes. When boating, keep your trash onboard. Dispose of it when you get back to shore.

Reduce, reuse, and recycle plastic. Try to find and use bags, packaging, and other items made of "green" plastic. This biodegradable plastic is made from cornstarch or other agricultural products. It decomposes over time.

According to David Helvarg, author of *50 Ways to Save the Ocean*, about 60 percent of trash left on beaches and 90 percent of trash found floating in the world's oceans is made up of plastic bags, food wrappers, bottles, fishing nets, fishing line, packing material, and balloons. (Many balloons released for special celebrations end up in the sea.) Helvarg says that the accumulation of everyday plastic in the ocean causes more damage than oil spills. Oil naturally dissolves over time. Plastic never does.

# FISH RESPONSIBLY 71

You can help protect marine environments by organizing a beach cleanup with your friends!

A study by the Algalita Marine Research Foundation found that parts of the North Pacific Ocean contain six times more plastic dust by weight than zooplankton, the basic fish food at the bottom of the marine food chain. Perhaps worse, fish often mistake pieces of plastic for food. They fill their stomachs with bits of plastic and starve. Pollutants absorbed by the plastic eventually poison such fish as tuna, billfish, and sharks. The toxins may also affect the reproduction and development of young fish and other marine organisms.

Avoid endangered and protected fish. Only fish for species that are plentiful in the ocean. If you accidentally catch the wrong kind of fish, release the fish without hurting it. When using live bait, use only species that already live in the fishery. Introducing foreign fish will upset the area's ecological balance.

Leave wildlife and its habitat undisturbed, including coral reefs and bird nests near fishing spots. If you notice damage or pollution caused by others, tell area authorities.

## DO NO HARM

Whether you're fishing on shore or at sea, there are lots of things to be mindful of. Though you may be an ethical fisher who would never dream of dumping trash into the water or beach, there are lots of ways to cause harm to the environment without meaning to! When we're focused on fishing, it can be easy to inadvertently damage a delicate ecosystem.

Here are some ideas of ways you can avoid harming marine habitats while you enjoy saltwater fishing:

## WATCH YOUR ANCHOR!

If you're saltwater fishing from a boat, take care to do your best to avoid harming both sea animals and habitats. Anchors can cause a lot of damage. Take care not to drop your anchor into a reef or seagrass bed. These are important habitats for saltwater species.

## RESPECT THE REEF!

Corals are very delicate and must be treated with the utmost care. These fragile creatures are critical to the survival of many marine species. If you're snorkeling or fishing near a reef, do not touch it.

## CARE FOR THE SHORE!

When fishing from the shore, be careful not to trample over native plants. These plants are essential to sand stability. Their roots hold it in place. Don't clear away dead plants either. Dead plants help restore nutrients to the shore environment.

## DON'T TAKE SOUVENIRS

When you're saltwater fishing, it can be tempting to collect natural souvenirs. It's best to leave coral, seashells, and other mementos where they lie. Taking pictures and making memories that will last you a lifetime are souvenirs enough!

# GLOSSARY

**angler:** Someone who fishes with a hook, or with a rod and line.

**artificial:** Made by people, not by nature.

**beacon:** A radio transmitter emitting signals to guide aircraft.

**buoy:** A floating object moored to the bottom to mark a channel or something else.

**conservation:** Efforts to care for the natural world.

**ethical:** Having to do with morals and principles.

**etiquette:** A set of social rules about the proper way of behaving.

**forecast:** Predicted weather conditions based on meteorological evidence.

**gadget:** An often small mechanical or electronic device with a practical use but often thought of as a novelty.

**radar:** A way of using radio waves to find distant objects.

**reel:** A device set on the handle of a fishing pole to wind up or let out the fishing line.

**regulation:** A rule or law that controls how something is done.

**wake:** The path of waves left behind a boat.

# For Further Reading

Brach, Kyle. *Deep-Sea Fishing*. Minneapolis, MN: Lerner Publishing Group, 2023.

Cermele, Joe. *The Total Fishing Manual: 318 Essential Fishing Skills*. San Francisco, CA: Weldon Owen, 2017.

Glitlin, Martin, and John Wilis. *Saltwater Fishing*. New York, NY: AV2, 2020.

Hemingway, Ernest. *The Old Man and the Sea*. New York, NY: Scribner, 1995.

Kinnison, Joe. *Next-Level Bass Fishing: Innovative Techniques That Have Elevated the World's Best Anglers to the Top*. New York, NY: Skyhorse, 2021.

Koretum, Frank W. *Intro to Bluefin Tuna Fishing for Kids*. Independently published, 2022.

Koretum, Frank W. *Intro to Saltwater Fishing for Kids*. Independently published, 2022.

Kreh, Lefty. *Lefty Kreh's Flyfishing in Salt Water*. Guilford, CT: Lyons Press, 2023.

McCoy, Matthew. *Knot Tying for Beginners: An Illustrated Guide to Tying the 25 Most Useful Types of Fishing Knots*. Independently Published, TangledTales Books, 2022.

Schwipps, Greg. *Fishing for Dummies*. Hoboken, NJ: John Wiley & Sons, 2020.

# For More Information

**American Sportfishing Association**
1001 North Fairfax St., Suite 501
Alexandria, VA 22314
(703) 519-9691
Email: info@asafishing.org
Website: asafishing.org
Facebook: /ASAFishing
The American Sportfishing Association is a trade association that represents the interests of the sportfishing community.

**Florida Fish and Wildlife Conservation Commission**
Farris Bryant Building
620 S. Meridian St.
Tallahassee, FL
(850) 488-4676
Website: myfwc.com
Facebook: /MyFWC/
Twitter: @MyFWC
This is a Florida state agency that regulates fish and wildlife resources.

**The International Game Fish Association**
300 Gulf Stream Way
Dania Beach, FL 33004
(954) 927-2628
Email: hq@igfa.org
Website: igfa.org
Twitter: @TheIGFA
Facebook: /TheIGFA/
The IGFA is a non-profit organization that records fishing accomplishments and promotes ethical fishing practices.

**National Fish and Wildlife Foundation**
1133 Fifteenth St. N.W., Suite 1000
Washington, D.C. 20005
(202) 857-0166
Email: info@nfwf.org
Website: www.nfwf.org/
Twitter: @NFWFnews
Facebook: /FishandWildlife/
The NFWF is an American government-backed agency that sustains and restores fish and wildlife habitats.

**National Oceanic and Atmospheric Administration**
1401 Constitution Ave. NW, Room 5128
Washington, D.C. 20230
(301) 427-8000
Email: outreach@noaa.gov
Website: www.fisheries.noaa.gov/topic/recreational-fishing-data/overview
Twitter: @NOAA
Facebook: /NOAAFisheries
The NOAA's purpose is to study and protect the climate, oceans, and coasts of the United States.

***Salt Water Sportsman***
517 N. Virginia Ave.,
Winter Park, FL 32789
(800) 759-2127
Email: SLScustserv@cdsfulfillment.com
Website: www.saltwatersportsman.com
Twitter: @SWSportsman
Facebook: /swsportsman
*Salt Water Sportsman* magazine offers info about the best fishing gear and boats as well as helpful tips from experts.

# INDEX

## A
Alaska, 13, 68

## B
backwater fishing, 4
bait, 23, 27, 28, 36, 39, 42, 44, 72
barracuda, 39
bass, 27, 39, 42, 47
billfish, 36, 72
birds, 44
bluefish, 36, 39, 47
boats and boating, 4, 9, 11, 12, 14, 15, 16, 17, 18, 19, 30, 33, 36, 37, 40, 42, 44, 54, 70, 73
bottom fishing, 26, 27, 36, 44
bream, 24
buoys, 17, 18, 19, 40

## C
California, 44, 66, 67
catch-and-release fishing, 50, 53, 54
chum, 27, 36, 44
cleaning fish, 54, 56, 57, 58
Coast Guard, U.S., 12, 16, 17, 67
cod, 4, 47
cooking fish, 58, 59, 60, 61, 69

## D
deep-sea fishing, 4, 42
drift fishing, 36, 44

## E
Endangered Species Act, U.S., 64
etiquette, 14, 15

## F
float fishing, 36, 39
Florida, 13, 45, 50
fly fishing, 36, 39

## G
gaffs, 30, 31, 54
GPS, 31, 33
grouper, 46, 50

## H
halibut, 4, 42
Hawaii, 40
herring, 54
hooks, 15, 22, 23, 24, 28, 30, 36, 39, 50, 54

## J
jetty fishing, 36, 38, 42
jigging, 36, 39

## L
licenses, 8, 69
line, 14, 15, 23, 24, 25, 26, 28, 30, 31, 39, 54
lionfish, 64, 65
Louisiana, 14
lures, 23, 27, 28, 29, 30, 31, 36, 39

## M

mackerel, 27, 47, 54
marlin, 4, 26, 29, 36, 39, 47
Massachusetts, 14

## N

New York, 13, 14
North Carolina, 14

## P

pier fishing, 4, 36, 42, 44, 45
plugs, 28, 30, 39
poppers, 28, 30

## R

reef fishing, 24, 53
reel, 22, 23, 30, 33, 39
rockfish, 39
rods, 9, 15, 22, 23, 24, 25, 26, 28, 30, 33, 39

## S

safety, 4, 9, 12, 15, 16, 17, 18, 41, 69
sailfish, 4, 36, 39, 47
seasickness, 11, 12
sharks, 4, 44, 47, 72
shore fishing, 16, 42
sinkers, 24, 39
snapper, 44, 46
snaps, 24
soft baits, 28, 30, 31
South Carolina, 42
spear fishing, 36, 39, 40, 41, 55
spinners, 28, 30
spoons, 28, 30

still fishing, 36, 39
structure fishing, 36
surf fishing, 4, 5, 36, 39, 42, 43, 47
swivels, 24

## T

Texas, 14
trolling, 24, 25, 26, 36, 37, 44
tuna, 4, 29, 36, 54, 64, 65, 72

## V

venting, 53
Virginia, 14

## W

weakfish, 27, 39

# ABOUT THE AUTHOR

Theia Lake is an avid writer and nature-enthusiast. She loves spending time outdoors and prefers the company of trees and wild things. Theia is a life-long student of science and the natural world. She lives in Buffalo with her children, cats, dog, and collection of natural treasures.

# ABOUT THE CONSULTANT

Contributor Benjamin Cowan has more than 20 years of both fresh and saltwater angling experience. In addition to being an avid outdoorsman, Cowan is also a member of many conservation organizations.

# PHOTO CREDITS

Cover Image Source Trading Ltd./Shutterstock.com; pp. 4-5 littlesam/Shutterstock.com; p. 5 Fabien Monteil/Shutterstock.com; pp. 6-7 joyfull/Shutterstock.com; p. 8 ArliftAtoz2205/Shutterstock.com; p. 10 Alexey Savchuk/Shutterstock.com; p. 11 Vladyslav Lehir/Shutterstock.com; p. 17 Nostagrams/Shutterstock.com; p. 18 Reagan V. Jobe/Shutterstock.com; pp. 20-21 Mindscape studio/Shutterstock.com; p. 22 orgbluewater/Shutterstock.com; p. 24 project1photography/Shutterstock.com; p. 26 Go2dim/Shutterstock.com; p. 28 AllMyRoots/Shutterstock.com; p. 29 lunamarina/Shutterstock.com; p. 32 lunamarina/Shutterstock.com; pp. 34-35 Jason Richeux/Shutterstock.com; p. 37 Fredrick Corey Chestnut/Shutterstock.com; p. 38 TamasV/Shutterstock.com; p. 40 Jacob Lund/Shutterstock.com; p. 43 iofoto/Shutterstock.com; p. 45 nyker/Shutterstock.com; p. 46 Rich Carey/Shutterstock.com; pp. 48-49 martinedoucet/iStock Photo; p. 51 Fabien Monteil/Shutterstock.com; p. 52 pshihtzu/Shutterstock.com; p. 55 Piotr Wawrzyniuk/Shutterstock.com; p. 57 Koliadzynska Iryna/Shutterstock.com; p. 58 Evgeny Litvinov/Shutterstock.com; p. 59 paullos/Shutterstock.com; pp. 62-63 FabrikaSimf/Shutterstock.com; p. 65 thediver/Shutterstock.com; p. 66 Sundry Photography/Shutterstock.com; p. 67 J.D.S/Shutterstock.com; p. 68 rafapress/Shutterstock.com; p. 71 Inside Creative House/Shutterstock.com.